Sherlock Holmes & Doctor Watson Annual

Published by GRANDREAMS LTD., 205/211 Kentish Town Road, London NW5. Printed in Holland.
ISBN 0 86227 016 2

THE CASE OF THE DEADLY SPECTRE

ALL KINDS OF THINGS... APPARITIONS, NOISES... TWO PEOPLE... NO THREE... BY JOVE! SIR OSWALD TAVERNER DIED OF FRIGHT IN THE PLACE! HE'S THE THIRD...
HOLMES? YOU'RE NOT LISTENING..?
AFRAID YOU'VE BEEN SOLD A PUP WATSON! THIS ISN'T 'LA LUNE'... IT'S A NASTY LITTLE WINE FROM 'LE SOLEIL NOIR' WITH A COUNTER-FEIT LABEL!
YOU'VE BEEN OVERCHARGED BY... OH, SEVERAL SHILLINGS A BOTTLE!
BY JUPITER! I'LL TAKE IT BACK FIRST THING IN THE MORNING AND COMPLAIN! IT'S CRIMINAL!
IT CERTAINLY IS, MY DEAR WATSON! BUT I'M AFRAID YOU WON'T HAVE TIME TO COMPLAIN...
I WON'T?
NO, WE'RE TAKING THE FIRST TRAIN IN THE MORNING TO COTLEY... NOW WHERE DID I PUT THAT TIME-TABLE...
COTLEY? SURELY WE'RE NOT GOING TO GET INVOLVED WITH ALL THAT SPIRITUALIST NONSENSE! GHOSTS AND TABLE-RAPPING...
I THINK IT'S A LITTLE MORE THAN THAT, WATSON... SOMEONE'S GOT SOMETHING TO HIDE... AND THEY'VE MURDERED THREE PEOPLE TO KEEP THE SECRET!
AND SO THE NEXT DAY FOUND US ON A TRAIN TO THE SOUTH COAST...
MURDERED, HOLMES? WHAT MAKES YOU SO SURE THEY WERE MURDERED?
SIR OSWALD TAVERNER WAS WITH THE SOCIETY FOR PSYCHICAL RESEARCH EVER SINCE IT BEGAN FIVE YEARS AGO... ONE OF THEIR MOST EXPERT INVESTIGATORS...
NOTHING WOULD HAVE FRIGHTENED HIM... LET ALONE TO DEATH!

COTLEY WAS TOO SMALL A PLACE FOR A STATION OF ITS OWN, SO WE HAD TO COMPLETE THE JOURNEY BY TRAP...
THAT'S THE MANOR-HOUSE, GENTLEMEN, UP ON THE CLIFF... TERRIBLE PLACE!
SO I HEAR... BUT PERHAPS YOU COULD PUT US DOWN AT THE LOCAL POLICE-STATION, DRIVER...
AND SOON...
GOOD DAY, GENTLEMEN! DON'T GET MANY STRANGERS IN THESE PARTS! LOST YOUR WAY, HAVE YOU?
NO, I THINK I'M IN THE RIGHT PLACE, CONSTABLE... MY CARD...
BLIMEY!
SORRY, SIR... JUST NEVER EXPECTED THE GREAT SHERLOCK 'OLMES TO COME TO COTLEY...! WHAT CAN I DO FOR YOU?
IT'S ABOUT SIR OSWALD TAVERNER... I WONDER IF YOU'D BE GOOD ENOUGH TO SHOW US THE BODY..?
WELL, IT IS STILL IN DR. MAURICE'S MORTUARY... BUT AS FAR AS I'M CONCERNED, THE CASE IS CLOSED. CERTIFICATE SAYS SHOCK AND HEART-FAILURE... THAT'S GOOD ENOUGH FOR ME!
I'M SURE DR. MAURICE IS RIGHT... BUT I'D JUST LIKE TO SEE FOR MYSELF...
AND THEN PERHAPS YOU COULD TAKE US UP TO THE MANOR-HOUSE...
SO YOU'LL BE WANTING TO TALK TO MR AND MRS VARLEY TOO, THEN...

AND SHORTLY...
NATURAL CAUSES, MR. HOLMES... ONLY MARK IS A SMALL BRUISE ON THE BACK OF THE NECK... MUST HAVE BEEN MADE WHEN HE FELL OVER!
NOT A BIG ENOUGH BRUISE TO SUGGEST HE WAS HIT?
OH, NO! ABSOLUTELY NOT!
NATURAL CAUSES... STAKE MY REPUTATION ON IT...
THANK YOU, DOCTOR...
I WONDER IF YOU'D EXCUSE US FOR A FEW MINUTES? DR. WATSON IS A SURGEON AND CAN GIVE ME ALL THE HELP I NEED...
BUT WHEN WE WERE LEFT ALONE...
LOOK, WATSON... THE BRUISE IS MOSTLY HIDDEN UNDER THE HAIR... BUT THERE IN THE CENTRE...
GOOD LORD! THERE'S A TINY PUNCTURE! MUST HAVE BEEN TOO SMALL TO BLEED MUCH...
BUT I WAS RIGHT... IT'S MURDER...
A LONG STEEL NEEDLE DRIVEN THROUGH THE SKULL, I'D GUESS... VERY NASTY... AND DIFFICULT TO DETECT...
NO, IT'S NOT ON, HOLMES... IT'D NEED A HAMMER...
WELL, BE THAT AS IT MAY... WE WON'T MENTION IT TO DR. MAURICE...
AND...
YOU WERE RIGHT OF COURSE, DOCTOR... NATURAL CAUSES! GOOD DAY!
CONSTABLE, I WONDER IF YOU COULD INTRODUCE US TO THE VARLEYS NOW?
OF COURSE, MR. 'OLMES... I'LL GET THE TRAP...

COTLEY MANOR ITSELF SEEMED TO HAVE FALLEN ON HARD TIMES... AND SO, APPARENTLY, HAD THE VARLEYS WHO OWNED IT...
USED TO HAVE A FINE STRING OF HORSES IN THAT STABLE MR. 'OLMES... BUT THEY ALL GOT SOLD WHEN THE FAMILY GOT INTO DEBT...
AND YOU SAY MR. VARLEY AND HIS WIFE ARE THE ONLY ONES WHO LIVE HERE NOW?
AND WHEN THE INTRODUCTIONS HAD BEEN MADE...
TERRIBLY DISTRESSING BUSINESS FOR YOU, OF COURSE... BUT I'M AFRAID I CAN ONLY SOLVE THE PUZZLE BY SPENDING THE NIGHT IN THE ROOM MYSELF...
OH, NO... WE COULDN'T ALLOW...
COME, COME, ANNA DEAR... THIS IS MISTER HOLMES, REMEMBER?
I DON'T HAVE TO WARN YOU OF THE DANGER... AND I'M AFRAID YOU'LL HAVE TO LOOK AFTER YOURSELF...
OUR BUTLER WAS THE FIRST TO DIE... AND WE HAD TO LET POWELL, THE ESTATE MANAGER, GO A COUPLE OF WEEKS PAST...
I UNDERSTAND, MR. VARLEY... BUT WHY DID POWELL LEAVE..?
THINK THE HAUNTING GOT TOO MUCH FOR HIM... TOOK TO DRINKING RATHER HEAVILY... I HAD TO SACK HIM IN THE END...
I'LL SHOW YOU TO YOUR ROOMS...
HOW LONG HAD HE BEEN WITH YOU?
THREE YEARS... LIVED IN THE FLAT OVER THE STABLES...
SO HE WAS NEVER IN THE HOUSE WHEN THE HAUNTINGS OCCURRED...
OH, WATSON... ASK CONSTABLE EDKINS TO WAIT... WE'LL BE GOING OUT AGAIN SHORTLY...

AND...
SO AT LEAST WE KNOW POWELL DIDN'T HAVE ANYTHING TO DO WITH ALL THIS...
PERHAPS, WATSON... WHERE'S HE LIVING NOW, CONSTABLE?
DOWN AT THE 'SKY LANTERN' INN, MR. HOLMES... IT'S IN THE VILLAGE...
IT WAS STILL MID-AFTERNOON WHEN WE ARRIVED, AND THE BAR WAS EMPTY...
HELLO, CYNTHIA! IS JIMMY POWELL ABOUT? LIKE A WORD...
DON'T TALK TO ME ABOUT JIMMY POWELL! I HAVEN'T SEEN THE DRUNKARD FOR THREE DAYS... AND HE OWES ME FOR HIS ROOM...
THIS IS MR. 'OLMES, FROM LONDON...
COULDN'T POSSIBLY HAVE A QUICK LOOK IN HIS ROOM, COULD WE?
WELL, I SHOULDN'T, BUT...
BUT THE LANDLADY DIDN'T TAKE MUCH PERSUADING...
NOW THAT IS INTERESTING...
WHAT IS IT, HOLMES?
'SOLEIL NOIR'...
AFTER THAT, HOLMES SEEMED TO LOSE INTEREST, AND WE LEFT...
BIG, POWERFUL FELLOW, JIMMY POWELL... IS HE?
WHY, YES, SIR, HE IS...
THINK I'LL TAKE A WALK ALONG THE BEACH... I'LL MEET YOU BOTH BACK AT THE MANOR AT NIGHTFALL...
AND CONSTABLE, MAKE SURE EVERY-ONE IN THE VILLAGE KNOWS I'M HERE...
HOLMES WAS BEING DELIBERATELY MYSTERIOUS, SO I DIDN'T QUESTION HIM... BUT I CONFESS I WAS WORRIED THAT NIGHT...
WELL NOW, I THINK I'LL JUST SIT HERE WHERE SIR OSWALD SAT... AND SEE WHAT HAPPENS...
BUT, HOLMES... IT'S DANGEROUS!
AND WHY ARE YOU WEARING YOUR OUTDOOR CLOTHES?

MIGHT GET **CHILLY**, LATER ON...
DON'T WORRY, WATSON...YOU CAN LOOK IN ON ME IN HALF AN HOUR! NOW, GO DOWNSTAIRS AND JOIN THE VARLEYS...
BUT A FEW MINUTES LATER...
AND BELOW, I HEARD A SUDDEN CRASH...
HOLMES!
GOOD GRIEF! HOLMES!
BUT...
HOLMES?
IT'S ALRIGHT, WATSON... I'M **SAFE!**
I **THOUGHT** I'D TRICK THE MURDERER INTO PLAYING HIS HAND IF THE WORD GOT ROUND THAT **I** WAS ON THE CASE...
MURDERER?
JIMMY POWELL, I BELIEVE...AND I IMAGINE HE'LL BE COMING OUT OF THE STABLE IN ABOUT **TWO MINUTES!**
WE'VE GOT TO **HURRY**, WATSON! I TRUST YOU'VE GOT YOUR **SERVICE REVOLVER** WITH YOU...

AND SURE ENOUGH, WHEN WE ARRIVED, BREATHLESS, AT THE STABLE DOOR...
STAND WHERE YOU ARE, POWELL! WE HAVE A GUN... YOUR STRENGTH WON'T DO YOU ANY GOOD NOW!
'STRUTH!
ALRIGHT... I'LL COME QUIETLY...
YOU WERE RIGHT, HOLMES... ONLY A STRONG MAN LIKE THIS COULD HAVE DONE IT! PUT THE CUFFS ON HIM, CONSTABLE... THE CHARGE IS MURDER!
AND SMUGGLING... YOU'LL HAVE TO FIND HIS ACCOMPLICES, TOO...
SMUGGLING?
AND AS HOLMES EXPLAINED WHAT HE HAD FOUND ON THE BEACH THAT AFTERNOON...
AN OLD SMUGGLERS' TUNNEL LEADS UP THROUGH THE CLIFF... IT HAD TO RUN TO THE MANOR HOUSE, THEN TO THE STABLE ...THIS IS WHERE THEY BROUGHT THE STUFF OUT...
THE WHOLE HAUNTING BUSINESS WAS JUST TO COVER THE SOUND OF THE BARRELS BEING DRAGGED THROUGH THE TUNNEL UNDER THE HOUSE...
AND THEY MURDERED EVERYONE WHO SAW THROUGH IT...
BUT... BARRELS OF WHAT, HOLMES?
OF 'SOLEIL NOIR'... THAT'S HOW POWELL GOT HIS WINE TO DRINK! HE SMUGGLED IT IN... PUT IT IN DIFFERENT BOTTLES...
SO ULTIMATELY, POWELL'S THE ONE WHO SOLD YOU A PUP AT THE WINE MERCHANT'S..!
C. 90
THE END.

Sherlock Homes has brought many remarkable villains to justice in his celebrated fictional career of fighting crime; colourful crooks created by the highly imaginative Sir Arthur Conan Doyle. Victorian England, however, produced a number of real life rogues and sensational crimes the equal of any fictional invention.

Charles Peace is a splendid example, an extraordinary villain known as the 'devil man' because of his ape-like face. A little, sinewy fellow, he was described by a contemporary as, "Almost a monkey of a man, with the remarkable power of pulling about and altering his features, so as to make his face unrecognisable to his relations and intimates."

A burglar and a murderer, Charlie Peace was a master of disguise and a clever actor. One day he would appear as a blind fiddler playing outside a mansion while he "sounded" the place for later robbery. Another day he would be a dark skinned pedlar, or an ex-sailor with an iron hook in place of a hand – a useful hook which he employed for climbing trees and walls to reach the window of a house he intended to rob.

He was incredibly tough and agile. Once, when attacked by a ferocious bulldog guarding a residence he picked up the snapping animal by its jaws with one hand and punched it insensible with the other. "I'm more than a match for any three men," he often boasted.

Peace began his long criminal career in 1850. After serving several prison terms he took to carrying a pistol in order to avoid further capture by the police. On an August night in 1876 he was departing from the scene of a burglary in Manchester when he was challenged by Constable Nicholas Cock. Peace levelled his gun and threatened the officer, "Stand back, or I'll shoot." When the policeman pulled out his truncheon and advanced, Peace shot him dead and escaped. A

Above: *Charles Peace robbing a house.* **Right top:** *Charles Peace, also known as the 'devil man' because of his ugly face and* **right bottom:** *Peace is captured.*

Vict
Vil

few months later he committed his second murder, shooting a man in Sheffield over an argument. Peace was now a much-wanted man with a £100 reward on his ugly head.

A cunning and elusive fugitive, he abandoned his old haunts and moved to London where he plagued the suburbs with a great number of burglaries. Charlie certainly had the cheek of the devil. One day he walked into a shop smoking an expensive cigar. "That smells like a fine cigar, Mr Johnson," said the shopkeeper (who knew Peace by that assumed name). "Where do you get them?" Charlie smiled and replied, quite truthfully, "I steal them." The shopkeeper laughed at the "joke" and also responded in jest, "Well then, perhaps you'd steal some for me." And Peace promised he would. Sure enough, a few days later the burglar presented the man with a box of fine cigars he had stolen from a house. The honest shopkeeper harboured not the slightest suspicion of the generous and apparently respectable Mr Johnson.

On a dark October night in 1878 two policemen on patrol in Blackheath noted a man acting suspiciously in a back garden. When challenged, the man fired three shots at the policemen, wounding Constable Robinson in the arm. The other policeman knocked the gunman to the ground and he was arrested. Taken to the police station, the man was

rian

ains

charged under the name of John Ward.

Inspector Bonney of the newly-formed Criminal Investigation Department (CID) of Scotland Yard was put in charge of the case. He had doubts about the true identity of the silent, dark skinned John Ward, who claimed to be a gipsy. Bonney soon discovered that the "gipsy's" swarthy appearance was the result of walnut juice rubbed into the skin. Further investigations revealed that the mysterious Ward was in fact the notorious Charles Peace.

Taken by train from London to stand trial at Sheffield Assizes, the agile "devil man" broke away from his guards and hurled himself through the open window of the train, which was moving at 45 mph. But he did not escape. When the train was stopped, the master crook was found injured and unconscious by the side of the track, Some months later he stood trial, was found guilty of murder and sentenced to death. Realising that he could not escape the gallows, Charles Peace made a complete confession of his crimes before he faced the hangman on 25 February 1879.

Murder by poisoning is an unusual crime today. But in Victorian times it happened a lot. Sherlock Holmes developed a wide knowledge of poisons and their peculiarities. The most infamous poisoner of the Victorian period was Dr William Palmer of Rugeley, in Staffordshire. He certainly murdered fourteen people in this manner, and possibly more, but at his trial he was charged with only three.

Born in 1824 Palmer inherited £7,000 (a small fortune in those days) when his father died in 1837. Palmer was a compulsive gambler and he soon wasted his inheritance on race horse betting. He got into debt and in order to obtain money he murdered. "It was the racing that did it," he commented after being found guilty in 1856. His victims included his mother-in-law, from whom he inherited property, his wife, whose life he had insured for £13,000, and a racing crony to whom he owed £800. Palmer poisoned them with considerable skill and patience and thus no suspicion was attached to him.

The deadly doctor was eventually brought to justice when he murdered John Parsons Cook, a racing friend of his who won the Shrewsbury Handicap with his mare Polestar in

November 1855. Cook won £2,000 on the race and celebrated his victory by giving a dinner party at a Shrewsbury hotel. Palmer was one of the guests. And he being sorely pressed at the time for debt decided to poison Cook in order to get his hands on the young man's winnings, part of which

he carried on him.

Cook, who had received several drinks from the hands of Palmer during the evening's merriment, was taken ill after the party. And naturally he was attended to by Dr Palmer. As Cook's condition became worse Palmer assumed complete control of the patient's treatment and business affairs, with the inevitable result that poor Cook died in terrible convulsions caused by strychnine poisoning. In an effort to obtain the balance of his victim's winnings. Palmer forged a document, this and several other factors brought suspicion on the doctor and he was charged with Cook's murder. When the bodies of some of Palmer's relatives were exhumed they were found to contain traces of poisoning.

William Palmer stood trial, was found guilty of murder and hanged on 14 June 1856. The story of "Palmer the Poisoner" ends with a grim jest. The good people of Rugeley, appalled at the unwelcome notoriety that their wicked doctor had brought on the respectable little town, approached the Prime Minister requesting permission to change the name of the place. "Certainly, you may," replied the Prime Minister, then added with a puckish sense of humour, "Why not call it after me?" The Prime Minister was Lord Palmerston!

The most sensational robbery of Victorian times was that of gold bullion and coin valued at £12,000 taken by subterfuge from the guarded van of a South Eastern Railway train. The crime baffled Scotland Yard. It had been carefully planned and carried out with daring and audacity. The robbers might have gone undetected but for the treachery of one of their number, which caused the thieves to fall out.

The Great Bullion Robbery was designed by two professional villains, Edward Agar and

William Pierce, who planned to steal the gold from the locked safes of the railway van while it was in transit between London and Paris. The idea was to substitute the gold with an equal weight in lead shot so that the robbery would not be discovered until the iron safes were opened in Paris.

In order to execute this bold and covert enterprise Agar and Pierce required the complicity of the train guard, James Burgess, and a well-placed railway clerk, William Tester. Both men agreed to take part in the robbery for a share of the gold. Between them the four men managed to obtain duplicates of three sets of keys to the bullion safes and, after waiting patiently for a full year, put their plan into operation on the night of 15 May 1855.

Having placed their carpet-bags full of lead shot in the guard's van, attended by Burgess, Agar, Pierce and Tester boarded the train at London Bridge Station. Just as the train was starting, Agar slipped unnoticed into the van where Burgess concealed him in a corner. As the train sped towards Folkstone, Agar opened the safes with the duplicate keys and removed the three boxes of bullion. With a mallet and chisel he deftly wrenched off the iron bands that bound the boxes, being careful not to make marks. Then, with a pair of pincers he drew out the nails that held the lids. Burgess helped him substitute the gold with the bags of lead shot. Agar replaced the nails and the iron bands, resealed the boxes with wax and locked them in the safe.

At different stops along the way, Tester, Pierce and Agar got off the train and each were handed a carpetbag (containing a portion of the plunder) by Burgess. The theft was not discovered until the boxes reached Boulogne, when they were found not to weigh exactly what they should (it had proved difficult for Agar to substitute the exact amount of shot). The police on both sides of the Channel were mystified. They had no clues, no suspects. Burgess was a trusted servant of the railway, and in any case, how could he have executed

Left top: *Dr Palmer in the dock during his trial for murder and* **above:** *the public execution of Palmer.* **Left bottom:** *The Great Bullion Robbery. Agar and Burgess open the chests of gold.*

such a professional crime?

Agar and Pierce lost little time in exchanging the bullion and gold coins for cash through their underworld connections. It seemed to be the perfect crime. However, good faith and trust are essential to partners-in-crime. William Pierce broke that trust and suffered the consequences. James Agar who now had plenty of money, foolishly tried to pass a forged cheque and was arrested in August 1855. He was convicted and sentenced to transportation for life.

On being convicted, Agar arranged with Pierce to invest his share of the bullion and pay Fanny Kay, the woman with whom Agar had been living, a regular amount. The greedy Pierce promptly welshed on the payments to Fanny Kay and appropriated Agar's share for his own use. In response to this treachery Fanny, who knew about the robbery, went to the police and put the finger on the three men. When Agar learned of Pierce's perfidy he volunteered to give evidence against his accomplices.

Pierce, Tester and Burgess were tried at the Old Bailey in January 1857. With Agar speaking against them they were found guilty. In passing sentence, the judge said: "A greater villain than you are, Pierce, I believe does not exist. The most severe sentence which the law allows me to pass upon you, however, is two years' hard labour. . .I regret I cannot pass a more severe sentence upon you, for you are worse than either of the others."

Tester and Burgess paid heavily for their betrayal of the railway company's trust. They were sentenced to transportation (to a harsh penal settlement in Australia) for a term of fourteen years.

Sherlock Holmes

The Case of THE CAT-BURGLAR

"Good morning, Lestrade!" Holmes said amicably, looking up from the breakfast table as our old companion from the Yard arrived with his customary haggard and careworn look. "And what can we do for you this morning?"

"As if you didn't know . . ." Lestrade replied, pulling up a chair uninvited and plumping down into it wearily.

"Why, how could I possibly know?" Holmes grinned as I poured the Inspector a cup of Darjeeling tea. There was a sparkle in his eye that I knew only too well. "All I can tell is that you've been up all night . . . again . . .".

"Too true . . . thank you, Doctor," Lestrade said to me, gulping down his tea gratefully. "It's this damnable cat-burglar! Struck again last night! The Eleventh time . . . my superintendent's having a fit!"

Before Holmes could reply, there was a knock at the door, and when I crossed the room to open it, there was a tall, militaristic gentleman standing there, wearing an impeccably-cut suit, his hair close-cropped to his head.

"Mr Holmes?" he asked, with a strong Germanic accent. I shook my head and showed him in. Holmes got to his feet to greet the man; Lestrade remained seated, looking at the newcomer with bleary-eyed indifference.

"My name is Staffel, Mr Holmes; a mere messenger, but I bring you a card and a letter from my superior . . ."

Staffel stood to attention with a slight click of his heels as he handed the letter over. Holmes looked briefly at the card, raised an eyebrow, and then opened the letter. He read it in silence, and then, ignoring Lestrade, replied: "I'll come immediately. Watson, be a good chap and see if you can find us a cab . . ."

"No need," Staffel said crisply, turning toward me. "I have a conveyance waiting outside."

"Excellent!" said Holmes, reaching for his hat and coat and indicating that I should do the same.

"Hold on, Holmes!" Lestrade said suddenly. "What about me . . . ?"

"Let yourself out, Lestrade," Holmes told him. "Have another cup of tea . . . then I'm sure you'll be wanting to get back to the Yard!" And we left him there spluttering.

Holmes said nothing of the contents of the letter while we rode, and Staffel simply said nothing at all. So it was with considerable surprise that I found our destination to be the Embassy of the Austro-Hungarian Empire, an imposing slab of masonry set in its own grounds not far from St John's Wood. The staff treated us with the utmost deference, and Staffel quickly led us to an office on the second floor. Then he withdrew, leaving us alone with two men.

"Mr Holmes!" said one of the men smoothly, extending a hand to my friend and then looking questioningly in my direction.

"My companion, Doctor Watson," Holmes introduced me. "A man of the utmost discretion . . . and a valuable assistant . . .".

"Very well . . ." the man replied, gripping my hand firmly. "Forgive me, Doctor, but this is a matter of some delicacy . . .". He turned back to Holmes. "I am Lutz, Secretary to his Excellency, the ambassador. It was I who sent you the letter . . . and this is Schmidt, in charge of security here. Please sit down, gentlemen. It was good of you to come so switfly."

Lutz appeared to be about forty, dark-haired and short of stature, but there was an assured confidence about him. I guessed his entire career had been spent in the diplomatic service; but Schmidt was obviously a military man, some ten years younger, tall and well-built, his hair cropped even closer than Staffel's, an arrogant twist to his lips. I had the distinct impression that, whatever this affair was about, he was quite confident of being able to sort it out himself, without bringing in any foreign outsiders.

"The point is, Mr Holmes," Lutz began, "that to our considerable embarrassment, we've been burgled . . .".

"I believe there have been a number of burglaries recently," Holmes said. "The victims have included some of the most notable people in London. I'm sure there's no need to be embarrassed . . .".

Lutz smiled slightly, then got to his feet, inviting Holmes to join him at the window. "The criminal appears to have got in here," he said raising the window sash. "There is a drain-pipe running down the wall here," he pointed, "and the window has been forced."

Holmes put his head out of the window briefly, looked at the pipe, and then gave a cursory glance at the window sill and sash. When he turned back to me, I could see that he was anything but pleased.

"Kindly ask your man Staffel to make ready the carriage, Herr Lutz," he said shortly. "We're leaving, Watson . . .".

"What?" cried Schmidt, leaping to his feet angrily. "Remember to whom you are speaking, Herr Holmes! We will not be treated with contempt!"

"It is nothing more than you deserve, sir!" Holmes replied, with a rare display of temper. "I merely return *contempt* for *deceit*!"

"I *told* you," Lutz snapped briefly at Schmidt, then turned back to us. "Please wait, Mr Holmes. We can explain everything . . .".

Holmes stopped, but it took a good deal more soothing talk from Lutz to persuade him to sit down again. There was still a good deal of tension in the air as the secretary began his explanation.

"First, I must take full responsibility for what has happened. Herr Schmidt, being in charge of security here, naturally thought that this was a matter he should sort out, without the assistance of outsiders. When I suggested that we call you, he naturally thought that it reflected badly on his own capabilities . . . so I suggested this small charade to prove to him that you were the right man for the job . . ."

"It was a very amateurish deception," Holmes said unforgivingly. "Anyone could have seen that the window was opened first, and then separate markings made on the sill and sash. The dent on the sill would have been alright, but the wood on the sash should have been forced outwards, not depressed inwards. Besides, the marks are an eighth of an inch out of alignment . . ."

I could see that Schmidt was astonished by this last remark, and after that he calmed down considerably. Lutz smiled again briefly, and then continued.

"Your reputation is very well-founded, Mr Holmes. You are right, of course. We have not been burgled . . . but the point is that we know who the burglar is. He is one of the Embassy staff, a man called Von Rotwang . . .".

"I see," Holmes said. "And he has been responsible for all eleven of the recent cat-burglaries?"

"Eleven?" Lutz looked surprised. "We had only heard of ten, but perhaps he was at work again last night. Needless to say, he is not here now, or we would have apprehended him ourselves . . .".

"You seem to know a lot about him . . ." I said. "May I ask how?"

"Indeed we do, Doctor," Lutz said, looking meaningfully in my direction. "As I said, this is a matter of some delicacy, and I must ask that anything I say to you is not repeated outside these walls . . ."

"Of course," Holmes assured him, and I could tell that his interest was now aroused to the point where his anger was rapidly fading. "Please continue."

"To put it crudely, Von Rotwang is a spy. All those skills and talents that he is now using so reprehensibly in the cause of theft, he learned from us. He was transferred here a few weeks ago from France, and I hasten to assure you, gentlemen, that he has never been engaged in any sort of activity contrary to the interests of Her Britannic Majesty's government . . .".

"Of course not," Holmes said coldly, and I could tell that he believed Lutz about as much as I did.

"Naturally, if your English police were to apprehend Von Rotwang, there would be a considerable scandal, and His Excellency the Ambassador wishes to avoid that at all costs . . ."

"So you're asking me to find him privately for you . . . and then hand him over to you?"

"Precisely," Lutz continued. "I assure you that he will be dealt with severely under Austro-Hungarian law. There is no question of his escaping lightly . . .".

"But what about the valuables he's stolen?" I asked. "Are we supposed to just forget about them?"

"Of course not, Doctor! Once they are found . . . well, an anonymous note to the police . . . and the criminal has, meanwhile, 'escaped' . . . you see what I mean?" He turned back to Holmes. "Well, Mr Holmes? My government would not be ungrateful if you were to undertake this case . . ."

"Perhaps . . ." Holmes pondered. "I have rather a full case-book at the moment. If I could let you know tomorrow . . ."

"Unfortunately, I have to return to Vienna tomorrow," said Lutz. "But Herr Schmidt will undoubtedly give you all the assistance you require . . ."

"Very well, I'll take the case!" Holmes said suddenly, with a firmness which even I found surprising. But before I could say anything, there was a knock on the door, and Staffel had returned. Lutz was called away to see the ambassador, leaving us alone with Schmidt.

"Well, this could be quite an interesting case, don't you think, Herr Schmidt?" Holmes said, suddenly affable. "Now, perhaps you could give me a description of this Von Rotwang. I shall need to know everything you can tell me about him. Do you have any of his documents?"

"We have his diplomatic passport here," Schmidt said. "He hasn't been back to the Embassy since he realised we'd discovered him."

"Excellent!" said Holmes enthusiastically. "May I see it?"

"Certainly. It's kept in Lutz's safe here." Schmidt got to his feet, pulling a large bunch of keys from his pocket, and went over to a wall-safe, previously hidden behind an old oil-painting.

"*You* have the key to *his* safe?" Holmes queried.

Schmidt smiled. "As you heard, Herr Lutz is leaving tomorrow, and his own documents have already been cleared out of the safe. As head of security, the key was handed over to me yesterday. Only Von Rotwang's documents remain . . ."

"Now isn't that interesting," Holmes said, as Schmidt opened the safe and handed him the passport. Holmes looked at it briefly, then handed it back to him. "I suggest, Herr Schmidt, that you put this passport in your pocket, and say nothing to anyone else . . . absolutely nobody . . ."

Schmidt gave him a querying look, but Holmes had already turned away by then, and had gone to the window. He glanced down at the Embassy grounds then turned back, all smiles.

"Doctor Watson and I must be going, Herr Schmidt," he said. "Perhaps you'd care to meet us at the Embassy Gate tonight as soon as it gets dark. We might have some news for you then . . ."

"But what about the description?" Schmidt began.

"Tonight will do. Now, where's that man Staffel of yours? We really must be going . . ."

Even Schmidt could see that there was no further point in holding us there, so he summoned Staffel and asked him to ready the coach. For myself, I could see the light of enthusiasm in Holmes' eye, and I was fairly certain that he was well on the way to solving the case already. But I also knew that he would only tell me about it when he was ready, and there was no point in pressurising him about it.

The carriage took us the short distance from St John's Wood to Baker Street in almost no time at all, but by that time Lestrade had long gone. Holmes spent ten minutes or so pacing up and down and puffing meditatively on his pipe, and then threw his coat on once more.

"Won't be long, Watson," he said cheerily. "I'm off to the Yard . . ."

"But Holmes!" I protested. "You gave your word not to mention this affair to anyone outside the Embassy!"

"And my word is my bond, Watson," he smiled. "But I must go and apologise to Lestrade for walking out on him this morning. Very rude of me . . ."

He was gone before I could question him further, and when he returned he spent the rest of the afternoon immersed in correspondence and other cases. I left him to it and got on with my journal.

At twilight, we took a pleasant stroll up to St John's Wood, and by the time we arrived at the Embassy it was completely dark; though a golden moon was just rising to give a faint illumination. By its light, we saw Schmidt waiting for us at the gate. Holmes greeted him quietly, and then, with great assurance, led us into the Embassy grounds. But instead of heading toward the main door, he took a diversion into the gardens, and then, to Schmidt's great astonishment, climbed into a huge rhododendron bush and sat down on the ground.

"What are we doing here, Herr Holmes?" Schmidt asked, as we joined my friend. Holmes silenced him, and then asked, in a whisper, if he still had the passport with him. Schmidt confirmed that he had, and Holmes nodded, satisfied.

"Your man Von Rotwang is an excellent safe-cracker, I assume," Holmes whispered after a while. "He is approximately five feet nine inches tall, has fair hair, a slim build, an athletic disposition and wears dark cloths . . ."

I glanced at Schmidt, and saw him staring at Holmes with an expression of wide-eyed astonishment that I had come to see very often.

"How . . . ?" he began, then stopped as he saw Holmes' imperturbable smile.

"Elementary, Herr Schmidt . . . if you look toward the Embassy building, you will see just such a person shinning up the drain-pipe toward Herr Lutz's office. If you take a couple of men, you can probably arrive in the office just as he's opening the safe. If you're too late, Watson and I will apprehend him on the way down . . ."

Schmidt disappeared at the run, and two or three minutes later we saw his face at the window, beckoning us to join him. When we arrived on the second floor, Von Rotwang was sitting in a chair, handcuffed, under the watchful eye of two muscular men, and the safe door was standing open.

"Herr Schmidt has your passport, Von Rotwang," my friend explained. "That is what you were after, wasn't it? You were going to leave the country tomorrow . . . with your very good friend, Herr Lutz . . ."

"Lutz?" Schmidt said, and I could see that events were moving too fast for him to keep up with.

"Friend and collaborator," Holmes continued. "I strongly suspect that Lutz has Von Rotwang's loot stored away somewhere, but I'll leave you to sort that out and return it, Herr Schmidt. Well, come on Watson, we must be off . . ."

"Wait," Schmidt said suddenly. "How . . . what makes you think Lutz had anything to do with this?"

"Simple," Holmes smiled. "It was his suggestion that you invent a silly game with the forced window, wasn't it? But it wasn't his intention to test me at all . . . rather he wanted to have those marks already there . . . so that when Von Rotwang forced his way in tonight to get the passport, no one would have noticed until he and his partner were long out of the country. You see, you got hold of his safe-keys just a little too soon . . . so Von Rotwang had to make one more burglary before he left . . . and that was one too many . . ."

Sherlock Holmes investigates....

THEN YOU PROBABLY KNOW AS MUCH ABOUT IT AS I DO! EVERY TIME I THINK I'VE FOUND SOME-ONE TO QUESTION... "NO SPEAK ENGLISH"!
BUT SURELY YOU MUST HAVE SOMEONE IN THE FORCE WHO CAN...
AH, CHINESE ISN'T A LANGUAGE... IT'S A DISEASE! IF YOU DON'T CATCH IT AT BIRTH...
I CAN'T EVEN FIND OUT WHO OWNS THE PLACE!
PERHAPS I CAN HELP YOU, INSPECTOR...
MY NAME IS YUEH... YUEH HENG-O...
MAY I COME IN?
YUEH. HSIAO-CHIEH, CH'ING TSO! WO SHIH SHERLOCK HOLMES!
HSIEH-HSIEH, HOLMES HSIEN-SHENG...
WHAT THE DEVIL...?
YOUR CHINESE IS IMPECCABLE, MR. HOLMES... BUT I THINK FOR THE INSPECTOR'S SAKE WE'D BETTER TALK IN ENGLISH...
WHY DIDN'T YOU TELL ME YOU COULD SPEAK CHINESE, HOLMES?
OH, IT'S JUST A SMATTERING, LESTRADE... A GENTLEMAN'S ABLE TO BE POLITE IN SEVERAL LANGUAGES...

ALRIGHT THEN, MISS! WHAT DO YOU KNOW ABOUT THE DRAGON'S PEARL RESTAURANT?
I OWN IT, INSPECTOR...
BUT PERHAPS I COULD ANSWER YOUR QUESTIONS LATER... MY IMMEDIATE BUSINESS IS WITH MR. HOLMES...
AND, IGNORING LESTRADE, MISS YUEH PULLED A PICTURE FROM HER BAG...
THIS WHITE JADE STATUETTE OF THE IMMORTAL LU TUNG-PIN WAS STOLEN LAST NIGHT. IT HAS BEEN IN MY FAMILY FOR SEVEN GENERATIONS...
IT IS, OF COURSE EXTREMELY VALUABLE ...AND THIS IS WHAT I WISH YOU TO FIND FOR ME, MR. HOLMES...
UNFORTUNATELY, I SUSPECT THE THIEVES WORK FOR A CERTAIN WANG T'U-FEI, HEAD OF THE WHITE TIGER TONG! A VERY DANGEROUS MAN...
THIS IS THE ADDRESS OF HIS CHIEF ESTABLISHMENT...
NOW HOLD ON, MISS! THIS IS A POLICE MATTER!
THE PLACE WOULD EMPTY IN SECONDS AT THE SIGHT OF A POLICE UNIFORM, INSPECTOR... AND I THINK MR. HOLMES IS RATHER MORE QUALIFIED FOR THE TASK THAN YOUR MEN...
JUST BECAUSE HE KNOWS A FEW WORDS?
ALRIGHT, HOLMES, I'LL GIVE YOU 24 HOURS... THEN I RAID THE PLACE!
THANK YOU, MR. HOLMES... IT'S BEEN VERY INTERESTING TALKING TO YOU!
NOW, INSPECTOR, LET'S GO AND ANSWER YOUR BORING QUESTIONS...
UNTIL THE SAME TIME TOMORROW, THEN, MISS YUEH...

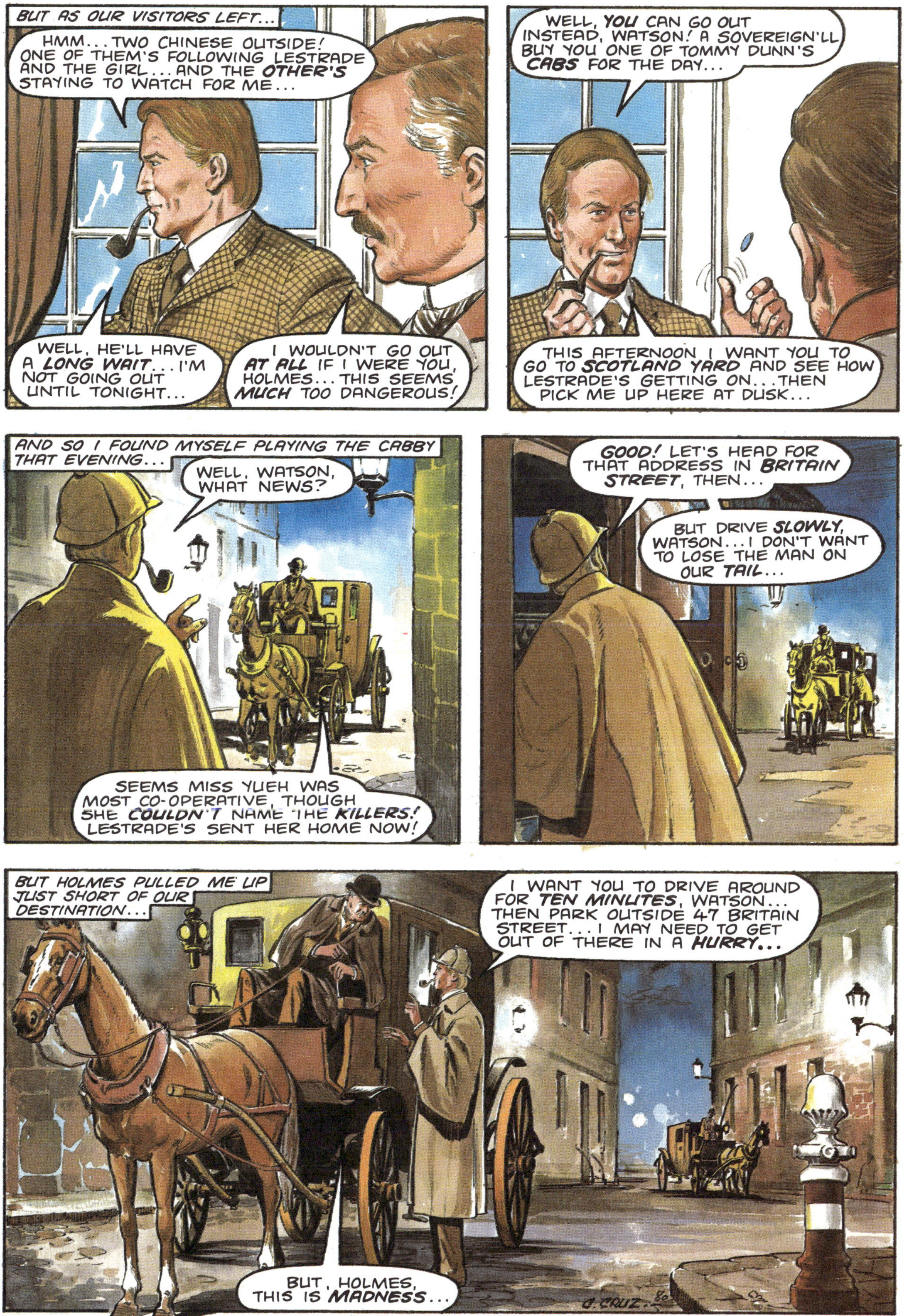
BUT AS OUR VISITORS LEFT...
HMM...TWO CHINESE OUTSIDE! ONE OF THEM'S FOLLOWING LESTRADE AND THE GIRL...AND THE OTHER'S STAYING TO WATCH FOR ME...
WELL, HE'LL HAVE A LONG WAIT...I'M NOT GOING OUT UNTIL TONIGHT...
I WOULDN'T GO OUT AT ALL IF I WERE YOU, HOLMES...THIS SEEMS MUCH TOO DANGEROUS!
WELL, YOU CAN GO OUT INSTEAD, WATSON! A SOVEREIGN'LL BUY YOU ONE OF TOMMY DUNN'S CABS FOR THE DAY...
THIS AFTERNOON I WANT YOU TO GO TO SCOTLAND YARD AND SEE HOW LESTRADE'S GETTING ON...THEN PICK ME UP HERE AT DUSK...
AND SO I FOUND MYSELF PLAYING THE CABBY THAT EVENING...
WELL, WATSON, WHAT NEWS?
SEEMS MISS YUEH WAS MOST CO-OPERATIVE, THOUGH SHE COULDN'T NAME THE KILLERS! LESTRADE'S SENT HER HOME NOW!
GOOD! LET'S HEAD FOR THAT ADDRESS IN BRITAIN STREET, THEN...
BUT DRIVE SLOWLY, WATSON...I DON'T WANT TO LOSE THE MAN ON OUR TAIL...
BUT HOLMES PULLED ME UP JUST SHORT OF OUR DESTINATION...
I WANT YOU TO DRIVE AROUND FOR TEN MINUTES, WATSON...THEN PARK OUTSIDE 47 BRITAIN STREET...I MAY NEED TO GET OUT OF THERE IN A HURRY...
BUT, HOLMES, THIS IS MADNESS...
J. CRUZ. 80

BUT I KNEW THERE WAS NO POINT IN ARGUING, SO I DROVE OFF, LEAVING HOLMES TO HIS FATE...
THEN...
I WANT A WORD WITH YOU, MY FRIEND! IT'S TIME YOU STARTED WALKING IN FRONT OF ME, INSTEAD OF BEHIND...
MMMF!
AND WE'LL HAVE THAT HATCHET OUT OF YOUR SLEEVE, TOO...
NOW, LET'S GO AND SEE YOUR BOSS...OR IF YOU DON'T UNDERSTAND ENGLISH...
K'AN NI-TI LAO-PAN! TSOU!
AND SOON, WITHIN THE PREMISES OF THE DREADED WHITE TIGER TONG...
PU-YAO TA! PU-YAO TA!
THAT'S RIGHT! YOU TELL THEM TO KEEP THEIR HATCHETS UP THEIR SLEEVES!
AND THEN...
AYAAH!
AH, MR. HOLMES! SUCH A DRAMATIC ENTRANCE! I KNEW MISS YUEH HAD HIRED YOU... BUT I CONFESS I DON'T KNOW WHY...
YOU HAVE SOMETHING SHE WANTS BACK, WANG... A CERTAIN JADE IMMORTAL!

YOU'VE COME HERE FOR A CHEAP BAUBLE THAT ONE OF MY MEN PICKED UP AS AN AFTERTHOUGHT?
IRONIC, ISN'T IT? AN IMMORTAL WAS A MAN SO HOLY HE'D LIVE FOREVER... AND BECAUSE OF HIM, YOU'VE GOT TO DIE..!
FOR HE WHO TREADS ON THE TAIL OF THE WHITE TIGER... GETS BITTEN!
PERHAPS:... BUT I'VE GOT TEETH, TOO!
AND BEFORE WANG COULD TAKE AIM...
NO... THE LAMP!
AAAH!
AND IN THE CONFUSION THAT FOLLOWED...

AND THE NEXT THING I KNEW...
WHAT THE DEVIL?
DRIVE, WATSON! DRIVE—OOOF!
AND SO IT WAS THAT NEXT MORNING...
YOU'VE GOT IT, MR. HOLMES! I HEARD THERE WAS SOMETHING OF A DISTURBANCE AT WANG'S ESTABLISHMENT LAST NIGHT...
YES... I HAD A FAIRLY INTERESTING TIME...BUT THERE IT IS, BASE AND ALL...
AND IT WAS THE BASE THAT MISS YUEH SEEMED MOST INTERESTED IN...
THERE'S SOMETHING MISSING!
YOU MEAN THIS, MISS YUEH? I THOUGHT THERE HAD TO BE MORE TO IT THAN A SIMPLE JADE STATUETTE...
THE SECRET COMPARTMENT WASN'T HARD TO FIND...
AND HERE ARE THE DETAILS OF YOUR OPIUM-SMUGGLING OPERATION... I IMAGINE YOU MUST HAVE BEEN MAKING RATHER A LOT OF MONEY OUT OF HUMAN MISERY...
I'M PREPARED TO KILL TO GET THAT PAPER BACK! YOU SHOULD HAVE STUCK TO YOUR TASK...
BUT FORTUNATELY LESTRADE AND I HAD HEARD EVERYTHING FROM THE OTHER ROOM...
NOW, THAT'S ENOUGH OF THAT, MISS!
LET ME GO, YOU PIG!
YOU WERE RIGHT, HOLMES... SHE DID KNOW ALL ABOUT IT..!
THAT'S WHAT THE RESTAURANT ATTACK WAS ABOUT... A GANG WAR OVER WHO CONTROLLED THE OPIUM RACKET...
STILL... I HATE TO SEE A PRETTY GIRL GOING TO PRISON...
BY THE TIME THEY LET HER OUT, SHE'LL NEED A WALKING STICK!
THE END.

Holmes' Victorian London
221B

JONES

COAL OFFICE
HARWITZ

The Case of THE SUSPECT SWAMI

Our visitor's name was Samuel Fowler, a middle-aged businessman with a slight Yorkshire accent and a brisk attitude, and he got straight to the point as soon as we invited him to sit down.

"I haven't come to see you on my own account, Mr Holmes," he began, "but rather about my sister. She's a few years older than I am, a spinster who lives alone, and daft as a brush! And I'm sure she's being defrauded by some scoundrel called Swami Khan . . .".

"Defrauded?" Holmes asked politely, as I offered our guest a cup of tea. "What makes you so certain?"

"What else could it be?" Fowler seemed surprised that there could be any possibility of doubt. "You know as well as I do there's nothing in this spiritualistic twaddle, Mr Holmes. All this mumbo-jumbo about the mystic East and Secret Masters living in the Himalayas! I don't believe it because I know it's impossible!"

I was inclined to agree with Fowler, but I noticed that Holmes merely smiled slightly without committing himself one way or the other.

"Trickery or not, these people can often bring a certain amount of comfort to the old and the bereaved," Holmes said after a moment. "But fraud is another matter entirely. Perhaps you'd better tell me more about this Swami Khan . . .".

"Claims to be an Afghan," said Fowler, "but he's the palest Afghan I've ever seen . . . skin's not much darker than yours or mine! He's actually had the gall to set up a 'consulting room' in Tottenham, as if he was some kind of doctor! Works there with an assistant called . . . what was his name? Tunn, I think that was it . . ."

"Then you've been there?" Holmes inquired. "And you've seen him at work?"

"I took Ellen there once . . . that's my sister's name by the way . . . when we couldn't find a cab for her. But I wasn't going to stay and have my intelligence insulted by cheap tricks and smooth talk . . ."

"So, you haven't actually seen him in action. May I ask if he charges for his 'services'?"

"Ah, well, that's the puzzling part, Mr Holmes. There's no charge as such, but he will accept voluntary contributions . . . though he puts a limit of one guinea on each offering . . ."

"That seems like quite a reasonable way to carry on," I remarked. "Hardly fraudulent . . ."

"But what else could it be but fraud, Doctor?" he asked me. "If the man's gone to these lengths with his tricks, what other reason could he have except to make money?"

"And when is your sister going to see him again, Mr Fowler?" Holmes said, and I could tell by his thoughtful tone of voice that he was beginning to become interested in the affair. Fowler pulled out his pocket watch and glanced at it briefly.

"Probably on her way there now," he said. "Goes to see him every Monday and Thursday morning apparently."

"Then I suggest we join her there," my friend said decisively, getting to his feet. Then he continued with great emphasis: "But, Mr Fowler, I must warn you that if I accept this case, I shall expect you to follow my instructions to the letter. We shall be going to this 'Consulting room' purely as interested parties. If you have any thoughts on trickery or the like, I'll thank you to keep them to yourself until we have left the premises. Otherwise I shall drop the case immediately . . ."

"As you wish, Mr Holmes, though I confess it'll be hard to keep a gag on my tongue. But I suppose you know best . . .".

"In matters like this, Mr Fowler, I think I do . . ."

Swami Khan's consulting rooms had once been a shop, I realised as soon as we arrived; the front sales-area having been converted into a comfortable reception room, with a row of chairs among the potted palms, and various mystic pictures on the wall, the significance of which quite escaped me, though I noticed Holmes looking at them with interest as we waited to be received. After a moment, a curtain was pulled back, and Tunn, a tall, elegantly dressed young man, came out to greet us.

"Mr Fowler . . . how pleasant!" Tunn said, proffering a hand which Fowler obstinately refused to shake. "The Swami told me to expect you, and your two friends . . ."

This seemed to take Fowler aback slightly. "Is my sister here?" he asked.

"Of course," Tunn replied. "Please come this way. But, gentlemen," and here he looked in our direction as well, "I must ask you to remain completely silent. The Swami is just going into trance, and it's most important that he should not be disturbed at such a crucial moment as this . . ."

We were shown through into a large room, where we found Ellen Fowler sitting alone on one of three rows of chairs. Swami Khan was lying on his side on a couch, his head on a pillow, the couch itself standing on a small raised platform like a stage. We could see little of his face, for a broad black blindfold covered his eyes, and I dark goatee beard sprouted from his chin. Incongruously, he wore an immaculate dinner-jacket, a bow-tie, and a turban. As we took our seats, Ellen Fowler looked sharply at her brother, then curiously at Holmes and I. But, following our instructions, we said nothing, and after a moment, the Swami sat up and faced us, still blind-folded.

"Welcome," he said, in a thick, heavily-accented, slurring voice. "Peace and blessings on you, Miss Fowler . . . Mr Fowler . . . Mr Holmes . . . Doctor Watson . . ."

I confess I was rather surprised by this, but Fowler seemed even more so. He began to splutter, and his sister silenced him with a sharp look. The Swami smiled.

"It is an honour to have such worthy guests," he continued, "and I must see if I can provide some demonstration fitting for the occasion . . ."

He lapsed into silence again for a moment, and I could see his entranced body shake slightly, his head nodding forward. When he raised his head again, there was a broad smile on his face.

"You live in a very pleasant house near Paddington, Miss Ellen," he began. "It has three floors, but the top one is rented to a young couple with a small child . . . a little girl. There are three aspidistra plants in your drawing room. A photograph of your lamented father over the mantlepiece. The curtains are of dark green velvet. On the window-sill is a Chinese willow-pattern vase, with chrysanthemums . . . two pink, three yellow. The carpet is Persian . . .".

The man continued in the same vein for two or three minutes more, and I could see Miss Fowler staring at him in open-mouthed astonishment. As for her brother, he too was looking surprised, but I could tell that he had long ago made up his mind that the man was a fake, and not even the most impressive demonstration in the world would convince him . . . or if it did, he would never admit it.

Done with cataloguing the contents of Miss Fowler's house, the Swami collapsed back on to the couch, shaking, and Tunn stepped forward on to the stage, sprinkling his face with water from a small jar. With a final shudder, Khan returned to normality, and sat up, removing the blindfold. He smiled broadly toward Miss Fowler, and our period of enforced silence came to an end.

"Wonderful!" she cried, getting to her feet as the Swami stepped down from the stage.

"A most impressive demonstration," Holmes remarked as the man came to join us.

"Thank you, Mr Holmes," the Swami replied, his voice still heavily accented, though no longer so thick and slurred as when he had been in trance. "Praise from such a worthy gentleman as yourself is praise indeed!"

"I'm sure I need hardly ask Miss Fowler whether you have ever visited her house," my friend continued.

"Why, of course he hasn't!" the lady replied, drawing another broad smile from the Swami.

"Bi-location is one of the arts I have studied with the greatest care," Khan continued, then noticed the puzzled expression on Fowler's face. "It means the ability to be in two places at once," he explained.

Tunn stepped forward and coughed softly to

gain the Swami's attention. "Mrs Dane is in the reception room . . ." he said.

"Forgive me," the mystic smiled. "I really cannot keep her waiting. Now, Miss Fowler, I should like you to go straight home, as swiftly as you can. Perhaps you will find a small surprise awaiting you . . .".

"Of course," she said, reaching into her purse and handing a few coins to Tunn. "Come along, Samuel. And thank you once again, Swami . . .".

"May eternal peace come to you all," Swami Khan said, bowing slightly and turning back to his couch.

Once outside, it was agreed that Holmes and I should accompany them back to Miss Fowler's house, though Holmes went to great pains to assure the lady that our interest was purely spiritual rather than investigative. According to instructions, the cabby took us to Paddington at a good clip, and there was no way anyone could arrive before us . . .

Nonetheless, as the cab drew up outside the door, there was Swami Khan standing there, his face wreathed in smiles, and he took Miss Fowler's hand and assisted her from the carriage.

"And now I really must return to Mrs Dane," he said, when we had all alighted. "I'll hope to see you on Monday, Miss Fowler. Good day, sirs!"

We were all rather too astonished to try to stop him or question him, and before we realised what was happening, he had walked away round the corner, ignoring the cab, and vanished from sight.

Entering the house, we found everything as the Swami had described, right down to the most minute detail. Miss Fowler seemed very pleased, and more convinced than ever.

"I only put those chrysanthemums in that vase this morning, just before I left," she said then went off to the kitchen to make a cup of tea.

"That was a fairly baffling display," I said, when the three of us were alone.

"Perhaps," Holmes said. "But while your sister is not here, let's get to business, Mr Fowler. Do you know if this Swami has provided any other evidence?"

"There was a letter last week," Fowler said. "Supposedly written by our dead father as 'proof of survival' after death. I looked at it, and it certainly *seemed* to be in his hand-writing, but . . ."

"And what did your father do?"

"Owned a textile mill up in Yorkshire . . . it's mine now. But he was quite a figure in the business in his time. Invented some sort of improvement to the looms . . . don't really know much about it myself; leave all that sort of thing to my manager . . ."

"And he patented this invention?"

"Of course! Practical Yorkshireman, my father was! But what's this got to do with anything, Mr Holmes?"

"Just that he would probably have written out the patent specification in his own hand," Holmes said thoughtfully. "So someone could go to the patent office, look at a sample of his hand-writing, and then a clever forger could have reproduced it . . ."

"So that might explain the letter," I said. "But what about the things we've seen today?"

Before Holmes could reply, Miss Fowler returned with a large tea-tray, and we all sat down together.

"I gather that Swami Khan does not charge for his services," Holmes said to the lady. "But has he ever made any other suggestions with regard to money?"

"Why, no," she said. "Not for himself anyway. He did suggest that when I'm . . . gone . . . I should leave my money to the Spiritual Research Foundation, and having no children, I'm seriously considering it; but apart from that, nothing . . .".

"And if it's not too impolite a question, how much would that amount to?"

"Several thousand pounds, Mr Holmes. But though I may be a middle-aged woman, I'm not silly. I checked, and the Swami has nothing to do with the organisation . . .".

We made small talk while we drank our tea, and then Holmes asked permission to look round the house. We left the lady in the drawing room, and Mr Fowler conducted us round. Everything seemed to be exactly as the Swami described.

"There's always the possibility that the Swami could be connected with this Foundation under an assumed name, or even through an intermediary," Holmes said thoughtfully, as we stood in the kitchen.

"Ah, good, you're coming round to my way of thinking at last!" Fowler said. He glanced toward the back door, then went over and picked up a key from the floor. "Must have fallen out of the lock, I suppose," he said, replacing it. "Surprised this Swami rascal didn't mention that too!"

A thought suddenly occurred to me. "Strange the way Khan didn't seem to recognise us when we arrived here, wasn't it, Holmes . . .?"

"Of course, Watson! You've done it again, my friend!" Holmes suddenly cried. "Quickly, let's go and find a cab! We'll get this affair sorted out in no time!"

Holmes said a brief goodbye to Miss Fowler, then rushed out, with her brother and I hot on his heels. Fowler continually asked him to explain, but Holmes, as was his custom, said nothing.

Our first call was to Scotland Yard, where Holmes persuaded Lestrade to delegate two constables to accompany us, and then we all returned to Khan's place in Tottenham.

There were no clients present when we arrived, and Holmes had no compunction about walking straight in. Tunn and Khan regarded the police with horror.

"Arrest these men, officers!" Holmes declared. "The charges are wilful deception, house-breaking, and, probably, conspiracy to murder. You'll find another room here somewhere, where, I wouldn't be at all surprised if you find a third man. Arrest him too!"

One of the constables set off to search the place, while the other and myself took charge of Tunn and Khan. Holmes led Fowler over to the stage and pulled the pillow off the couch.

"You see?" he said, pointing. "There's a speaking-tube built into the couch, which doubtless leads to the room the constable's checking. That's how information was passed to Khan, while he was supposedly lying there going into trance. That's how he knew that Watson and I, and yourself, had arrived here this morning. Tunn went off to the other room and told him. Ah . . ."

Holmes paused as the door opened, and the constable returned with a third man. And I stared at him in astonishment.

"Swami Khan's twin brother," Holmes announced.

"But how . . .?" Fowler began, totally baffled.

"Quite simple," Holmes explained. "Let me reconstruct this morning's events for you. Khan's twin waited outside your sister's house until he saw her leave, then broke in, picking the lock of the kitchen door. He made an inventory of the house's contents, then let himself out the same way. But while it's simple enough to unpick a lock, doing it up again requires the key. So he took it out with him, locked the door, and slid the key back underneath . . .

"Then he rushed back here, read out the information to Khan over the speaking tube, and then departed again immediately . . . so he could be standing there waiting to greet your sister on her return. But of course, he had already left here when we arrived, which is why he didn't recognise us!"

"But conspiracy to murder?"

"Once your sister had changed her will, how long do you think it would have been before she had an accident? No, I think you called me in just in time, Mr Fowler . . ."

Holmes and Watson

THE CASE OF
THE KRIS OF DEATH
IT WAS LATE ONE NIGHT WHEN LESTRADE CALLED US TO THE MAYFAIR MANSION OF THE FLOOHEY FAMILY. IT WAS MURDER SURE ENOUGH, BUT CAN YOU SPOT THE CLUES WHICH HELPED HOLMES SOLVE THE CASE?
THERE HE IS, HOLMES... THE HONOURABLE PATRICK FLOOHEY... DECEASED! AND WITHIN THE LAST HOUR, TOO...
NOTHING'S BEEN TOUCHED... THIS IS EXACTLY THE WAY THE BUTLER FOUND HIM...
SOMEONE STABBED HIM IN THE BACK WHILE HE WAS GOING THROUGH THE FAMILY ACCOUNTS...
AND BY THE LOOKS OF THINGS, THE LATE MISTER FLOOHEY WAS A VERY RICH MAN...
THE MURDER-WEAPON'S A MALAYAN KRIS... ONE OF THAT PAIR ON THE WALL...
SO WE KNOW WHERE THAT CAME FROM...

I CAN'T FIND ANY SIGN OF FORCED ENTRY, AND NO ONE'S LEFT THE PREMISES...
SO THE MURDERER MUST STILL BE HERE...
THEN I SHALL WANT TO SEE EVERYONE... FAMILY AND STAFF...
THEY'RE ALL HERE IN THE DRAWING ROOM... I'LL INTRODUCE YOU...
FRANCIS FLOOHEY, THE DEAD MAN'S YOUNGER BROTHER...
FRANCIS' WIFE, VICTORIA...
ANNABELLE SWANN, THE DEAD MAN'S FIANCEE...
ROGER BOWEN, THE EXPLORER...
THE DOMESTIC STAFF, MR GUDGER THE BUTLER, MRS PRITCHETT THE COOK AND JOSEPHINE JALAQUE THE HOUSEMAID...
AND THE HEAD OF THE FAMILY, MRS FLOOHEY...
C. CRUZ
YOU ALONE ARE NOT A MEMBER OF THE HOUSEHOLD, MR BOWEN... MAY I ASK WHY YOU'RE HERE..?
PATRICK AND I WERE MEMBERS OF THE EXPLORER'S CLUB... I RETURNED FROM AN EXPEDITION LAST WEEK...
AND I WAS HOPING TO PERSUADE PATRICK TO FINANCE ANOTHER TRIP...
AND WHERE HAVE YOU BEEN TRAVELLING?
I'VE JUST COME BACK FROM THREE YEARS IN THE MALAYAN JUNGLE...
I THOUGHT I WAS COMING BACK TO CIVILISATION... NOT THIS!

MALAYA? YOU'RE FAMILIAR WITH THE KRIS, THEN?
I'VE SEEN IT IN USE, YES...
THIS MUST BE VERY DISTRESSING FOR YOU, MRS FLOOHEY, AND IT'S RATHER LATE...
MISS JALAQUE, PLEASE TAKE YOUR MISTRESS TO HER ROOM. WE WON'T NEED TO TROUBLE HER AGAIN TONIGHT.
PLEASE RETURN AS SOON AS YOU'RE READY, MISS JALAQUE...
NOW, LESTRADE, I WANT TO CHECK SOMETHING IN THE STUDY AGAIN...
HMM... JUST AS I THOUGHT...
CHEER UP, LESTRADE, WE'RE NEARLY THERE...
WE ARE? YOU MIGHT BE... BUT I'M BAFFLED...
THEN...
YOU MUST ALL BE FINDING THIS EXTREMELY UPSETTING, BUT I WON'T KEEP YOU MUCH LONGER...
MR GUDGER, PERHAPS YOU SHOULD POUR EVERYONE A BRANDY...

OH, AND POUR ONE FOR YOURSELF, MRS PRITCHETT AND MISS JALAQUE...
COME NOW, MR. HOLMES... WE DON'T ALLOW THE SERVANTS TO DRINK...
BUT I THINK WE MIGHT MAKE AN **EXCEPTION** UNDER THE CIRCUMSTANCES, MR FLOOHEY...
BESIDES, I WANT TO MAKE A LITTLE TOAST...
TO THE DEFEAT OF CRIME... AND THE SPEEDY APPREHENSION OF THE MURDERER...
I'LL DRINK TO THAT!
VERY WELL, LESTRADE... BRING YOUR OFFICER IN HERE...
WE'LL NEED HIS HANDCUFFS WHEN YOU ARREST THE MURDERER...
YES, HOLMES HAD SOLVED THE CASE ALREADY! BUT DID YOU SPOT THE **CLUES** THAT GAVE HIM HIS LEAD? AND **WHO** WAS THE MURDERER?
FIND OUT OVERLEAF...

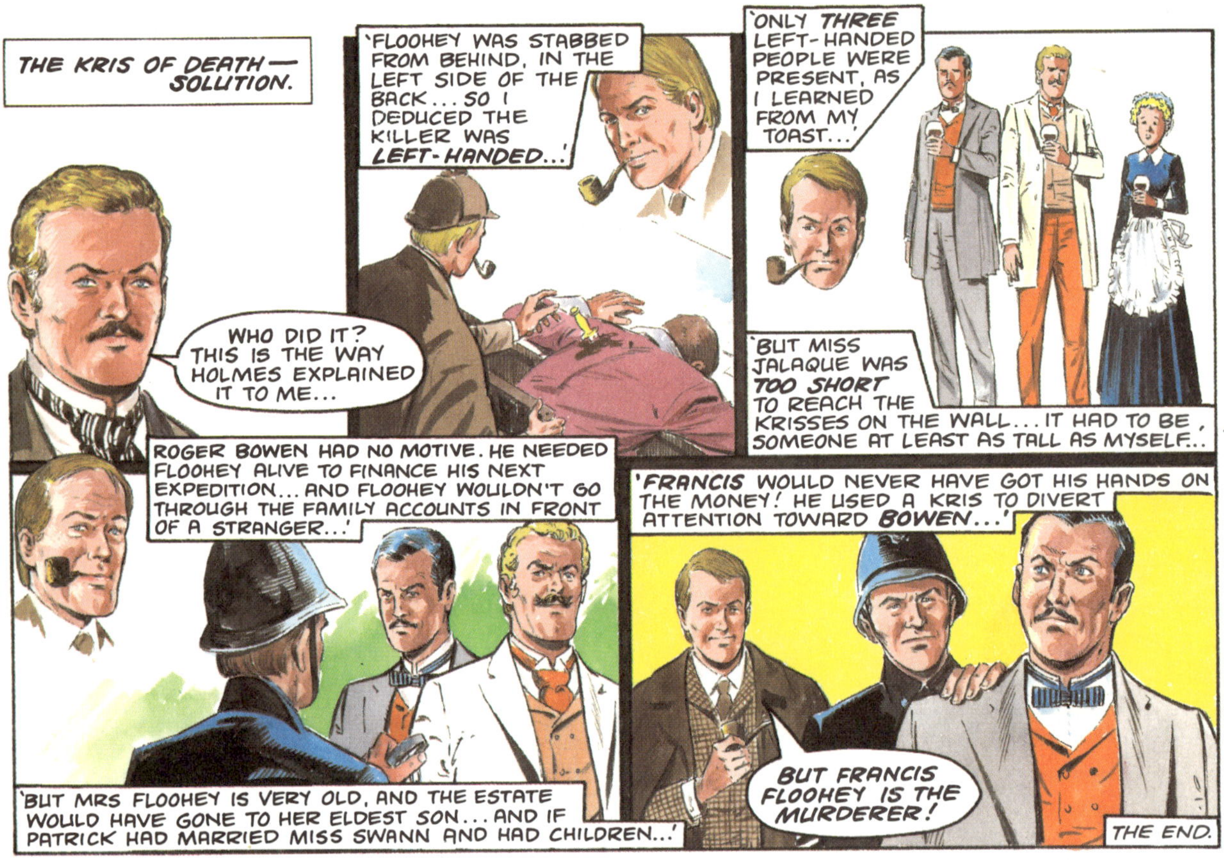
THE KRIS OF DEATH — SOLUTION.
WHO DID IT? THIS IS THE WAY HOLMES EXPLAINED IT TO ME...
'FLOOHEY WAS STABBED FROM BEHIND, IN THE LEFT SIDE OF THE BACK... SO I DEDUCED THE KILLER WAS LEFT-HANDED...'
'ONLY THREE LEFT-HANDED PEOPLE WERE PRESENT, AS I LEARNED FROM MY TOAST...'
'BUT MISS JALAQUE WAS TOO SHORT TO REACH THE KRISSES ON THE WALL... IT HAD TO BE, SOMEONE AT LEAST AS TALL AS MYSELF...'
ROGER BOWEN HAD NO MOTIVE. HE NEEDED FLOOHEY ALIVE TO FINANCE HIS NEXT EXPEDITION... AND FLOOHEY WOULDN'T GO THROUGH THE FAMILY ACCOUNTS IN FRONT OF A STRANGER...'
'BUT MRS FLOOHEY IS VERY OLD, AND THE ESTATE WOULD HAVE GONE TO HER ELDEST SON... AND IF PATRICK HAD MARRIED MISS SWANN AND HAD CHILDREN...'
'FRANCIS WOULD NEVER HAVE GOT HIS HANDS ON THE MONEY! HE USED A KRIS TO DIVERT ATTENTION TOWARD BOWEN...'
BUT FRANCIS FLOOHEY IS THE MURDERER!
THE END.

Inspector Lestrade

Famous Victo

Inspector William Tanner of Scotland Yard was one of the first detectives to win public fame. It was he who hunted down the perpetrator of the first train murder in this country. On 9 July 1864 the body of an elderly man named Thomas Briggs was found in a first class compartment of the North London Railway. He had been battered to death with his own walking stick and robbed of money and a gold watch and chain.

Investigating the scene of the crime, Tanner found that the hat in the compartment did not belong to the victim, it was most certainly the murderer's hat. In his haste to get away the killer had taken Mr Briggs' hat in mistake for his own. The murderer's hat was a foreign type with a low crown, in contrast to the high hat then commonly worn in England.

Inspector Tanner picked up the fugitive's trail at a jeweller's shop in Cheapside, owned by a Mr Death, whose unusual and chilling name caught the public imagination. The wanted man had sold Mr Death his victim's gold watch chain. Further inquiries revealed the fugitive's name to be Franz Muller, a young German tailor. The detective then discovered that Muller had left England on the sailing ship *Victoria,* bound for New York. It seemed that Muller had eluded the law, for once in the United States he could easily disappear in that vast country.

Tanner, however, decided to pursue his man. Accompanied by another detective, he took passage on the steamship *City of Manchester,* which set out across the Atlantic five days after the *Victoria* had sailed. But Tanner's steam packet was much faster than the sailing ship and he arrived in New York three weeks ahead of the *Victoria.*

...an Detectives

The inspector arrested the surprised Muller before he could set foot in the United States. When Tanner examined the German's hat (in fact Mr Briggs' hat) he found that its crown had been cut down to alter its appearance. Muller was also in possession of his victim's gold watch. Brought back to stand trial for murder, the evidence against him was sufficient to bring a verdict of guilty and he was hanged.

Inspector Tanner won public acclaim for his dramatic race across the Atlantic, and Muller started a fashion – for young blades adopted the distinctive headgear with the low cut crown known as the "Muller hat".

Inspector Walter Melville was a celebrated Scotland Yard detective of the 1890s, noted for his physical courage and resourcefulness. At one time he was on the trail of a notorious French gunman who had managed to gain entry into England while on the run from the French Surete, when the man pulled out a gun and started to shoot at the detective. In the face of flying bullets, Melville rushed the gunman and knocked him flat, then snapped on the handcuffs and took him into custody.

Another time, when a foreign monarch was paying a visit to London, word reached Scotland Yard that a malcontent from the same country, now living in London, intended to injure or kill the royal visitor in a coming procession. Melville was sent to deal with the potential trouble-maker, who worked as a cellarman for a wine merchant. The detective asked the wine store proprietor for a certain brand of champagne; the proprietor told his foreign cellarman to take Melville into the wine vault to select his champagne.

The unsuspecting malcontent unlocked the cellar and went inside. Melville remained by the door. "What's that wine over there?" asked the detective, pointing to the far end of the vault. As the man walked towards the spot, Melville stepped smartly outside the cellar and locked the door. "There you stay, my lad, until the procession is over." Inspector Melville had settled a potentially explosive international incident, quietly and quickly.

A fine example of dogged detective work was the Case of the Tell-Tale Chisel. It was solved mainly by Sergeant Cobb of M Division of the Metropolitan Police, a determined and conscientious officer who, convinced that he knew the identity of the guilty man, pressed on – in spite of opposition from his superior – to prove his case.

The story starts on a foggy December night in 1882. Police Constable Cole was patrolling the Dalston area of London when he caught a man about to climb through a window of a house. He tackled the intruder, who shot the policeman dead and ran off. Two women witnessed the murder and hurried to the nearest police station. Sergeant Cobb went to the scene of the crime, and on discovering several clues left by the murderer in his hasty escape, was certain that he knew the identity of the burglar-gunman.

One of the clues was a wide-brimmed hat. It just so happened that a few hours before the shooting, Sergeant Cobb had noticed a man loitering in the vicinity of the crime. The man, a smalltime crook named Thomas Henry Orrock, was well known to Cobb. Orrock had been wearing a wide-brimmed hat. The sergeant reported this to Inspector Glass, his immediate superior in charge of the case. Glass had Orrock brought in for an identity parade. But the two women witnesses failed to recognise the suspect as the man they saw struggling with the policeman. Orrock was discharged and soon after he vanished.

Cobb was still convinced that Orrock was the killer. His insistance annoyed Inspector Glass, who firmly believed in nothing

Left: *Inspector William Tanner of Scotland Yard, one of the first detectives to win public fame.* **Above:** *Tanner crossed the Atlantic in a steamship to arrest Franz Muller.*

but hard evidence and came to view Cobb's obsession with Orrock as a nuisance. A few months later the inspector was involved in more immediate matters and seemed to lose interest in the case. But Sergeant Cobb would not give up. He examined another clue, a chisel dropped by the burglar-killer at the scene of the crime when he fled. The blade, near the handle, had some scratches on it, which appeared to spell "rock". To Cobb this was another link with Orrock, but he would have to prove it.

The sergeant sleuth questioned many petty villains who knew Orrock and about a year after the crime one man gave him an important lead. He had been on Tottenham Marshes with Orrock when the latter was testing a revolver he had recently obtained. This incident had taken place a few weeks before the murder of Constable Cole. The man took Cobb to the marshes and showed him the tree that Orrock had used for target practice. The sergeant dug out the bullets in the tree and on examination they were found to be the same calibre and make that had killed the policeman.

When Cobb reported the matter of the scratched chisel and the bullets to Inspector Glass he could not ignore such evidence. Glass relunctantly pursued the clue of the chisel and eventually his men found a hardware shop that sharpened tools. "I scratched 'rock' on that blade," said the shopowner, "to identify the customer who brought it in. It's short for Orrock." The inspector was now convinced that Sergeant Cobb had been right all along. But Thomas Henry Orrock had vanished. He could be abroad, he might even be dead? Inspector Glass grew weary of looking for him.

Sergeant Cobb thought long and hard about the possible whereabouts of the missing man. Finally he came up with the one place that a policeman would not think to look – in prison. A convict answering to Orrock's description, but not his name, was found in Coldbath Fields prison; he had been there for two years, entering shortly after the murder of Constable Cole. But was it really Orrock?

An identification parade was held and Sergeant Cobb immediately recognised a prisoner as Thomas Henry Orrock, who confessed to shooting Constable Cole and was duly hanged. Sergeant Cobb was publicly acclaimed for his devotion to duty and promoted.

Real life detectives bear little resemblance to Sherlock Holmes, whose immense knowledge, expertise in many fields, and keen analytical mind enables him to solve the most mystifying crimes. There was, however, one brilliant detective the equal of the great fictional sleuth. He was the Frenchman Dr Edmond Locard, born in 1877, who became the Director of the Scientific Police Laboratory in the city of Lyons.

Locard was a leading pioneer of modern criminology who employed science, medicine, and his considerable intellect to solve many difficult crimes. His knowledge on various subjects was as wide as that of Sherlock Holmes. He was an expert on botany, poisons, graphology (the study of handwriting), forgery, fingerprints, stamp collecting, music, and the vagaries of human nature. We have only space to relate two of his numerous cases.

Locard's penetrating eagle eyes missed nothing. While investigating a particular murder, he was walking through a police station when he stopped in front of a tramp who had been arrested for vagrancy. He noticed on the man's dirty coat a tiny piece of rare dandelion.

MULLER'S LAMENT.

Tune.—"The Roving Gardener."

My name is Francis Muller, an unhappy little man
So listen to my trials and my troubles;
It's true what the poet says, this life is but a span,
And the world is made up of air bubbles.
So being short of tin, I thought some cash to raise,
Likewise to cut a figure in this nation,
But my sad capers now has got me in a mess,
And brought me too my present situation.

Oh, dear! have I got a chance
To escape from my present situation?
I am afraid Dickey Calcraft will teach me for to dance,
Which causes me great agitation.

They say I did a deed, all in the railway train,
And another person's property did borrow;
But whether true or not, I am sure you can't me blame,
If I speak not of that tale of sorrow.
Then I thought I'd take a trip to America,
And being a bit of a soldier,
I thought I would join the Federal army—
But the sequel it has to be told, sir.

I sailed in the Victoria,—just to take a trip,—
Just thinking all was right and tight, sir;
But when they found in England I had given them the slip,
They soon was down upon my flight, sir;
For the English deteclives knew too much for me,
They are too cute in this nation;
They soon made the sea far too strong for me,
So I long'd to change my situation.

I tried to make myself agreeable while I was on board,
And the passengers they thought I was a rum one
They said a murderer was on board, when the wind it roar'd,
Or else that old Nick he was coming;
I tried to get a bite, but found I was not right,
Just to amuse the passengers,
In a twinkling of an eye to put out of sight,
Five pounds of German sausages.

I said I was a tailor, I was upon my word,
When they said where is your bodkin and needle?
Says I, they are all right, along with my sleeve board,
So I managed them for a-while to wheedle.
Just to make a shift I had to sell my shirt,
It is truth now what I do tell ye,
For it is a fact, I cared not for my back,
So as I feasted well my belly.

I thought I was all right, but I found out my mis-take,
So it took me by surprise, it must be granted;
When Inspector Tanner came on board, and said, your arm I'll take,
For I tell you, Mr. Muller, you are wanted,
To the Police Court they took me in New York,
Where amongst the Yankees I was mingling,
Then aboard the Etna they did me escort,
And brought me back to old England.

I own I was a flat to keep the watch and hat,
It has give my bowels such a shaking,
Just when the rolls are drawn, on some fine morn,
I shall be strung up like a flitch of bacon;
So all young men take advioe by me,
No matter what country or colour,
For honesty is the best of policy,
Take warning by poor Francis Muller.

London:—Printed for the Vendors.

Left: *Contemporary broadsheet about the Muller case.* **Above:** *Franz Muller, who committed the first train murder in Britain in July 1864 and* **below:** *Inspector Walter Melville.*

He questioned the tramp on his movements and the man claimed that he had never been near the scene of the murder. But when Locard examined the fragment of dandelion under the microscope he was certain that the tramp was lying. The rare plant grew only in the field where the victim had been found. Faced with this scientific evidence the man confessed to the crime.

When Lyons was plagued with a series of baffling burglaries, Dr Locard was called in to solve the mystery. The thief worked in daylight and left no apparent clues. Some of the open windows, through which the thief always gained entry, were on the top floors of high apartment buildings, which even the most agile cat burglar would find difficult if not impossible to reach.

Locard thoroughly examined all the scenes of the thefts. The only clues he could find were remarkable fingerprints on the window panes, remarkable because they had no human pattern and all the ridges ran vertically. For several days Locard's department endeavoured to solve the puzzle of the curious fingerprints. It was the dilligent doctor who provided the answer. "They must belong to an ape or a monkey," he said. "Monkeys can climb and they can be trained to steal."

When an assistant asked him how they would find the right monkey, Locard replied that in his opinion monkeys could be identified by their unique fingerprints just as humans can. And Locard proceeded to have every monkey in the city, zoo and private, fingerprinted, with the result that the monkey burglar was found to belong to an Italian organgrinder, who confessed that he had trained the animal to steal.

For nearly eighty years the large, turreted building known as Scotland Yard, on the Thames Embankment, served as the bastion of law and order, the headquarters of the Metropolitan Police. Honest citizens of gaslit, foggy London were proud of the place that housed the finest detectives in the world. Crooks and villains feared and respected the granite castle from which, sooner or later, dedicated officers would swoop and bring them to justice.

But why call a police headquarters "Scotland Yard"? The origins go back to the Middle Ages when an area of land at the Charing Cross end of Whitehall was known as "Scotland" because it was here that buildings were established to house Scottish kings visiting English monarchs in the Palace of Westminster. Part of the area came to be called Scotland Yard.

It was in this district, early in the 19th century, that a large house at No. 4 Whitehall Place was taken over as police headquarters. The Police Office occupied the rear part of the premises and backed on to Scotland Yard; the policemen took to calling their station by that name. Scotland Yard became so closely associated in everybody's mind with police headquarters that the name was never changed.

With the growth of the Metropolitan Police (founded by Sir Robert Peel in 1829) new central offices were needed. A site had been acquired for a national opera house, but when this project failed, the new Scotland Yard, largely built of granite quarried by Dartmoor convicts, was erected instead. The building on the Embankment was completed in 1890 and served as Metropolitan Police headquarters until 1967 when the organisation moved to a purpose-built concrete and glass complex at Broadway, Victoria, known officially as New Scotland Yard.

Above: *Inspector Frank Froest and* **right:** *A view of Scotland Yard in 1898.*

The "Yard" is world famous for the excellence of its detectives. And the reputation is well deserved. However, when plain clothes detectives were first introduced in 1842 they were greeted with much hostility and suspicion, generally viewed as "government spies" threatening the liberties of Englishmen. The original Detective Office consisted of two inspectors and six sergeants. Because they were few in number and not specially trained, these early detectives were not very successful. The department grew and training was introduced. In 1850 Charles Dickens wrote an article called "The Modern Science of Thief-Taking" for his journal *Household Words,* based on his own interviews with men of Scotland Yard's detective force.

The Criminal Investigation Department (CID) was first organised within the Metropolitan Police in 1878. Its members were handpicked experienced officers. An early CID success was the capture and identification of notorious burglar and murderer Charles Peace (see the article VICTORIAN VILLAINS). The high quality and bulldog determination of the CID men in Victorian times are best embodied in the stalwart figure of Inspector Frank Froest, who combined physical toughness with a sharp, resourceful brain.

In 1892 Froest was sent to the Argentine to bring back the bigtime swindler Jabez Balfour. Attacked by Balfour's bodyguard, big Frank fought his way out with his fists, taking the wanted man with him, and boarded a train for Buenos Aires. When the firemen, bribed by Balfour, refused to stoke the boiler, the intrepid detective stripped off his coat and shovelled the coal himself. After more trouble with Balfour's cohorts, and the Argentine police (Britain had no extradition agreement with the country), Froest managed to get his prisoner on a ship and brought him back for trial. Balfour was sentenced to fourteen years and Inspector Froest was promoted to superintendent of the CID.

The greatest advance in

The Story of Scotla

criminal detection was the introduction of the fingerprint system of identification, officially adopted by Scotland Yard in 1901. This infallible method of identification (each person's fingerprints are unique, different from those of any other person) was championed, developed, and introduced by Sir Edward Henry when he was Assistant Commissioner in charge of the CID. The new system, however, was greeted with suspicion, many critics doubted Henry's claim of positive identification from such prints.

The first great "fingerprint case" in which the system proved its worth came in 1905. The case concerned the murder and robbery of a shopkeeper at Deptford, South East London. CID men searched the scene of the crime and found an empty plundered cashbox. At the Yard's laboratory the cashbox was dusted with fine powder and closely examined under a powerful magnifying glass. The searching lens revealed a single, broad, clear thumbprint. It was compared with the small number then on record, but it did not tally with any of them.

Further investigation into the crime brought forth two prime suspects, the Stratton brothers. When asked to make an inked impression of their thumbprints, the brothers smiled at the novel idea. But the joke was on them. The tell-tale print on the cashbox proved to be that of Alfred Stratton. Both were implicated in the callous crime and both were later hanged. Following this historic case the fingerprint system was adopted by all the world's police forces. Today there are over two million prints on record at New Scotland Yard.

The Flying Squad (C8) was formed in 1919 in order to have a mobile body of experienced detectives for special duty to deal with particular outbreaks of crime. In the early 1920s, with the development of radio communication and the use of fast cars (with police drivers trained on the famous Brooklands racing track) the Squad "flew" all over London in successful pursuit of crime. A journalist on a popular newspaper coined the dashing name "Flying Squad" and it has stuck ever since. It is also known as the "Sweeney" (from the Cockney rhyming slang "Sweeney Todd") and the "Heavy Mob".

Today there are 13 Branches of the CID at New Scotland Yard. C1, the Central Office, is the traditional centre of the Department. It is from C1 that three of the most famous Squads at the Yard operate: the Murder Squad, the Serious Crime Squad, and the Bomb Squad, the latter formed in 1972 to deal with the increasing use of explosives by political extremists. The Serious Crime Squad was formed to deal with the rise of organised crime, and so successful has it been In this field that it has earned the nickname "Gang-busters."

The Murder Squad has three teams of experienced detectives, headed by a Detective Chief Superintendent, constantly on 24-hour standby duty to deal with requests from Overseas or Provincial Forces. Scotland Yard has no authority to investigate crimes outside the Metropolitan area unless its services are specially requested by the local police of the district.

The Metropolitan Police District is divided into 15 Divisions each under a Commander. The Divisions are each divided into sub-divisions, with a Chief Superintendent in charge, and then further split into sectional police stations under the control of a Station Officer. Including the river stations of Thames Division, there are 190 police stations and offices serving the public and all are linked by telephone, and many by teleprinter, to each other and to New Scotland Yard, the historic heart and nerve centre of law and order in the great metropolis.

It is interesting to note that the present New Scotland Yard, designed as the world's most modern crime-fighting fortress, still retains its traditional cable address: "Handcuffs, London."

d Yard

THE CASE OF THE MISSING MUMMIES

A WONDERFUL COLLECTION YOU HAVE HERE, AHMET BEY... AND ALL EXCAVATED BY YOURSELF?
NOW HERE'S A FINE CASE...
AH, YES... THAT ONE ONLY ARRIVED THIS MORNING... HELD UP BY GRASPING OFFICIALS AT THE ALEXANDRIAN DOCKS...
BUT HERE IS THE GOLDEN FLOWER OF MY COLLECTION... THE BODY OF NEPT, COURT-MAGICIAN TO THE PHARAOH, EVEN BEFORE THE MIGHTY PYRAMIDS WERE BUILT...
HMM... A MAN OF SOME SUBSTANCE IN HIS TIME...
TRUE... BUT RATHER SHRUNKEN NOW...
GIVES ME THE CREEPS... I'VE HEARD OF THE CURSE OF THE PHARAOHS... BUT IT'S EVEN WORSE WITH A BLACK MAGICIAN...
AH, ONLY THE SUPERSTITIOUS PEASANTS OF MY WRETCHED LAND BELIEVE SUCH THINGS, INSPECTOR... BUT THIS IS THE GREAT CITY OF LONDON...
BUT EVEN IN CAIRO SOME OTHERWISE INTELLIGENT PERSONS TRIED TO STOP ME BRINGING NEPT HERE! MAY THE DESERT SAND SCOUR THEIR BONES WHITE!
QUITE... HMM, THAT'S STRANGE... I EXPECTED PROFESSOR KEIGHTLEY TO BE HERE...
HRMMF! THE ESTEEMED KEIGHTLEY AND I DO NOT SEE... HOW YOU SAY?... EYEBALL TO EYEBALL OVER CERTAIN TECHNICAL MATTERS...
AH, DOCTOR HIGGINS..!
DOCTOR HIGGINS WAS THE MUSEUM CURATOR...
I'M GLAD YOU TAKE AN INTEREST, MR HOLMES... I FEEL MUCH SAFER ABOUT SECURITY WITH YOU IN TOWN...
I HOPE YOU WON'T HAVE ANY NEED OF MY SERVICES, DOCTOR...
NOW, WHERE'S WATSON? WE REALLY MUST BE GOING...

BUT, BEFORE THE SUN HAD RISEN AGAIN...
WHAT'S THIS, CONSTABLE? IT'S ONLY SIX IN THE MORNING...
I'M SORRY, DOCTOR... BUT IS MR HOLMES HERE? INSPECTOR LESTRADE WANTS HIM AT THE MUSEUM...
AND SO...
YOU INCOMPETENT SON OF A BEETLE! THE FLOWER OF MY COLLECTION... AND SOME-ONE'S PLUCKED IT FROM YOUR PIFFLING, RICKETTY MUSEUM!
I TAKE IT FROM THAT, THE MUMMY OF NEPT IS MISSING, LESTRADE..?
AND THE MUMMY NEXT TO IT... THOUGH WHY ANYONE WOULD WANT TWO OF THE HORRORS IS BEYOND ME...
THE NIGHT-GUARD'S MISSING, TOO...
I THINK YOU MAY HAVE MISCOUNTED, LESTRADE... PERHAPS IT'S THREE MUMMIES MISSING... AND ONE GUARD...
...FOUND...
BY THE PROPHET!
GOOD LORD! IT'S THE CURSE... I KNOW IT IS!

NO, IT WAS A HUMAN HAND THAT DID THIS, LESTRADE... YOU'VE GOT YOURSELF A MURDER CASE AFTER ALL...
BUT SURELY THIS IS IRRELEVANT... HE WAS ONLY A GUARD!
BUT NEPT... HOLY NEPT...
YOU'VE GOT TO GET NEPT BACK, MR HOL'MES! I CANNOT OPEN MY EXHIBITION WITHOUT HIM, EFFENDI!
AND I CANNOT WORK WITHOUT BEING LEFT ALONE, AHMET BEY! EXCUSE ME...
WHERE'S DOCTOR HIGGINS?
AND SO DOCTOR HIGGINS GAVE US THE USE OF HIS OFFICE...
THIS IS TERRIBLE, MR HOLMES... I LOCKED JONES IN HERE LAST NIGHT MYSELF... AND I'M THE ONLY ONE WITH THE MASTER-KEY...
HMM... MAY I SEE THAT KEY?
INTERESTING...
MAY I HANG ON TO THESE FOR THE MOMENT? AND ON YOUR WAY OUT, COULD YOU ASK LESTRADE TO COME IN...
WELL, HOLMES?
OUR FIRST CLUE, LESTRADE... THERE ARE TRACES OF SOAP ROUND THIS KEY...
SOMEONE'S MADE AN IMPRESSION... AND THEN, NO DOUBT, A DUPLICATE!
SO IT MUST BE AN INSIDE JOB, THEN! I'LL START QUESTIONING THE MUSEUM STAFF!
LET'S SEE, THERE MUST HAVE BEEN AT LEAST TWO OF THEM TO CARRY OFF THOSE MUMMIES!

GOOD SHOW, LESTRADE! QUESTIONING THE STAFF WILL GIVE YOU SOMETHING TO DO WHILE WATSON AND I ARE OUT SOLVING THE CASE...!
BUT...YOU MEAN... **HOLMES**! WHERE ARE YOU **GOING?**
TO SEE A MAN ABOUT A MUMMY! BE BACK LATER...
AND EVEN I DIDN'T KNOW WHERE WE WERE GOING, UNTIL...
GOOD MORNING! IS PROFESSOR KEIGHTLEY AT HOME?
NO, SIR, I'M AFRAID HE'S OUT LECTURING...HE'LL BE BACK ABOUT FIVE!
MY NAME'S **SHERLOCK HOLMES**... I'LL LEAVE YOU MY CARD...
I WANTED TO ASK HIM ABOUT A CERTAIN EGYPTIAN CALLED **NEPT**... I'LL WRITE IT ON THE BACK OF THE CARD... AND PERHAPS I COULD COME AND SEE HIM THIS EVENING...
CERTAINLY, SIR... I'LL TELL HIM YOU CALLED...
NOTHING MORE WE CAN DO ABOUT NEPT NOW... THE QUESTION IS, WHY STEAL THE **OTHER** MUMMY AS WELL?
YOU MEAN THE OTHER **TWO** MUMMIES!
NO, I RATHER THINK THERE WAS ONLY **ONE**...
WHAT? BUT...
LET'S GO AND SEE **AHMET BEY**...
SO, SOON, IN A PLUSH HOTEL SUITE...
I'VE COME TO SEE YOUR MASTER...MY NAME'S HOLMES...
I DON'T THINK HE UNDERSTANDS, HOLMES...
AHMET BEY! **AHMET BEY!**

AND THEN...
FORGIVE ME, HONOURED GUESTS! I WAS JUST TALKING TO THOSE DELIGHTFUL MINXES, MY WIVES...
SO YOU HAVE YOUR HAREM WITH YOU?
INDEED, YES! WAIT OUTSIDE, KEMAL! NOW, GENTLEMEN, HAVE YOU CHEERING NEWS OF NEPT?
NOT YET I'M AFRAID... BUT I WANTED TO ASK YOU ABOUT THE OTHER MUMMIES...
AH, THEY ARE OF NO CONSEQUENCE BY COMPARISON, MR HOL'MES... I HAVE A DESCRIPTION OF THEM HERE SOMEWHERE... YOU CAN HAVE IT...
WE LEFT SOON AFTERWARDS, THEN, LATER THAT DAY, RETURNED TO PROFESSOR KEIGHTLEY'S...
YES, SIR, HE'S HOME... BUT HE'S GOT SOMEONE WITH HIM AT THE MOMENT...
OH, AND WHO MIGHT THAT BE?
DON'T KNOW, SIR... I WAS OUT ON AN ERRAND AND THE PROFESSOR MUST HAVE LET HIM IN HIMSELF...
THEY WERE ALREADY UPSTAIRS WHEN I CAME...
AYAAAUUGH!
BY JOVE!
AND, UPSTAIRS...
DEAD! STABBED IN THE BACK... JUST LIKE POOR JONES AT THE MUSEUM!
AND THE KILLER MUST HAVE ESCAPED THROUGH THAT WINDOW...
GO AND GET LESTRADE, WATSON... I'LL LOOK AROUND...

I FOUND LESTRADE STILL AT THE MUSEUM, NOT FAR AWAY...
BUT WHY, HOLMES? WHY KEIGHTLEY?
BECAUSE OF WHAT HE HAD TO TELL ME... FORTUNATELY, HE WAS GOING OUT AGAIN, SO HE STARTED TO WRITE ME A NOTE...
COME ON, LESTRADE... I'LL TAKE YOU TO YOUR MURDERER...
AND, SHORTLY AFTER...
SO KEIGHTLEY THOUGHT THE MUMMY OF NEPT WAS A FAKE? BUT...
HOLD ON, HOLMES... THIS IS WHERE AHMET BEY'S STAYING...
7 POLICE
POLICE
PRECISELY, LESTRADE... I HOPE YOUR MEN CAN HANDLE THEMSELVES IF THINGS GET... STICKY...
THERE'S YOUR MURDERER, LESTRADE... KEMAL THE NUBIAN...
AND AHMET BEY PUT HIM UP TO IT!
ARE YOU MAD?
"NO, NOT MAD... KEMAL WAS HIDDEN IN THE MUMMY-CASE WHICH 'ARRIVED LATE'. THAT WAS HOW HE GOT IN AND STABBED JONES... THE DUPLICATE KEY WAS JUST TO GET HIM OUT WITHOUT RAISING THE ALARM..."
"A MAN LIKE KEMAL COULD HAVE MANAGED BOTH MUMMIES ...THEY'RE VERY LIGHT... JUST DRY SKIN AND BONE! AND I SUSPECT HE KILLED KEIGHTLEY TOO..."